Fish

BY MICHELLE LEVINE

Amicus High Interest is an imprint of Amicus
P.O. Box 1329, Mankato, MN 56002
www.amicuspublishing.us

Library of Congress Cataloging-in-Publication Data
Levine, Michelle, author.
 Fish / Michelle Levine.
     pages cm. – (Animal kingdom)
 Summary: "An introduction to what characteristics animals
in the fish animal class have and how they fit into the animal
kingdom"—Provided by publisher.
 Audience: K to grade 3.
 Includes bibliographical references and index.
 ISBN 978-1-60753-473-0 (library binding) —
 ISBN 978-1-60753-620-8 (ebook)
 1. Fishes—Juvenile literature. I. Title.
 QL617.2.L48 2015
 597–dc23
                                    2013031406

Editor: Wendy Dieker
Series Designer: Kathleen Petelinsek
Book Designer: Heather Dreisbach
Photo Credits: Alamy 5, 18, 22, 26, 29; Corbis, 13, 17, 25;
Shutterstock, 21; Superstock, cover, 6, 8-9, 10, 14

Printed in the United States of America at Corporate Graphics
in North Mankato, Minnesota.

10 9 8 7 6 5 4 3 2 1

Table of Contents

What Is a Fish?

Swish! A trout swims down a stream. Zoom! A shark chases its ocean meal. Nearby glides an eel. And a ray skims the sea floor below. These animals do not all look alike. But they belong to the same animal class. They are all fish.

 Are whales fish? What about dolphins?

Sharks are some of the biggest fish in the ocean.

 No, they are not fish. Whales and dolphins are actually mammals. They live in water, but they have to breathe air like we do.

This colorful mandarinfish lives in warm water.

Fish are alike in many ways. They all live in water. And they all have a backbone. Most fish are also **cold-blooded**. Their bodies match the temperature around them. You are warm-blooded. Your body temperature stays the same. It does not change in the heat or cold.

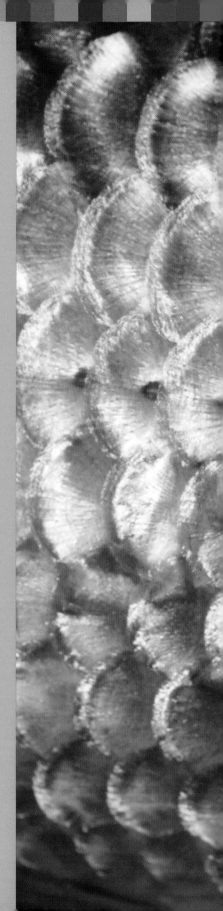

Most fish are covered with **scales**. Some fish have big scales. Others have small ones. Some scales are smooth. Others are very rough.

Another thing that fish have in common is how they move. They swim. They use their fins to get around in water.

Scales cover a fish's body.

9

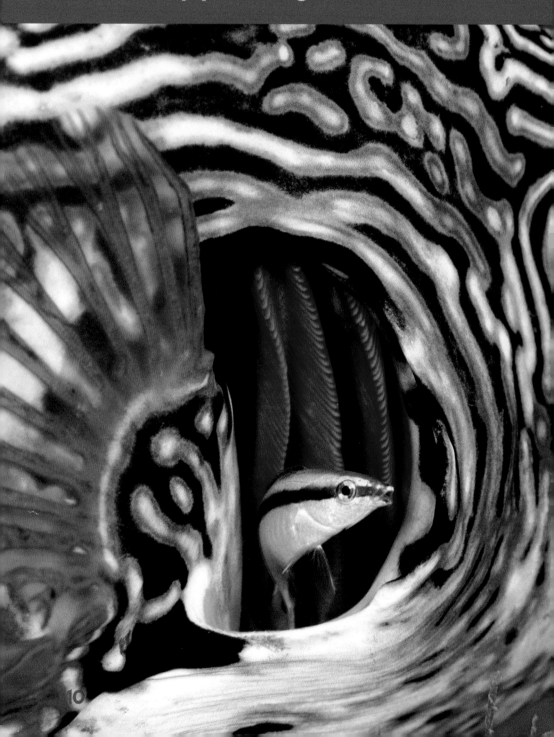

A small cleaner wrasse cleans
a map puffer's gills.

Fish need oxygen to live. So do you! You breathe air to get oxygen. Fish breathe underwater. They gulp water with their mouths. Then they breathe out the water through their **gills**. The gills are on either side of a fish's head. The gills take in the oxygen.

Eat or Be Eaten

Crunch! A shark bites into its meal. Most fish have strong jaws and sharp teeth. Some fish are **carnivores**. They hunt and eat other animals. Some fish are **herbivores**. They eat only plants. Other fish are **omnivores**. They eat both plants and animals. And some fish are **scavengers**. They eat animals that have already died.

 Which fish is called the "trash can of the sea"?

Whale sharks are omnivores.
They eat small fish and tiny plants.

 Tiger sharks. They eat just about anything.
They even eat trash!

It's hard for a predator to catch just one fish in a school swimming together.

 How does the blowfish stay safe?

Fish have many **predators**. So how do they stay safe? A crocodile fish blends into the sea floor. Its color matches its surroundings. Herrings swim together in **schools** to stay safe. A catfish's spines keep predators away. Still other fish make electricity. They give predators a painful shock. Ouch!

It puffs up like a balloon near predators. Then it's too big to eat.

Living in Water

Fish live almost anywhere there is water. They live in cold, warm, and hot places. Tunas live in the salty ocean. Others, like trout, live in lakes and rivers. Salmon start their lives in freshwater. They move to the ocean after hatching. They only return to freshwater to lay eggs.

This perch lives in a lake.

A fish's body is made for swimming. Its shape lets it move easily through water. Most fish are also covered in a slippery slime. The slime helps them move smoothly. Fins are important too. A fish uses tail fins to push through water. It uses other fins on its back to change direction or stay balanced.

A fish's fins are made for moving fish through the water easily.

Fish use their senses to survive in water. Some fish have very good eyesight. Others have a strong sense of smell. Many fish also have good hearing. But you can't see their ears. They are inside their bodies.

Fish have one extra sense you don't have. They can feel movements in water. This special sense tells them if animals are near.

 Do fish have a sense of taste?

Take a look at this fish's eye.
Some fish see really well.

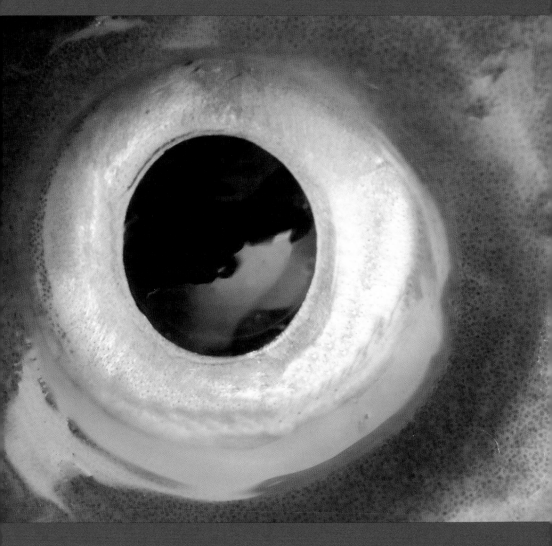

 Most fish are like you. They taste with their
mouths. But some fish can taste with other body
parts. The threadfin fish can taste with its fins!

Fish lay hundreds of eggs at one time.

Making Babies

Male and female fish come together to **breed**. Different kinds of fish breed at different times of year. It could be spring, summer, fall, or even winter.

Most female fish lay their eggs in water. Then male fish **fertilize** the eggs. And a baby fish begins to grow inside each egg.

Fish eggs are tasty treats for predators. Some fish hide their eggs in sand or mud underwater. Others guard their eggs. But most fish do not protect their eggs. They just lay a lot of them. The ones that don't get eaten hatch. Out comes a baby fish.

 What is the most eggs a fish can lay?

These baby salmon swim together to stay safe.

 The ocean sunfish lays up to 28 million eggs at a time.

Bears catch fish for a tasty meal. Yum!

 How many kinds of fish are there?

Fish in the World

Fish are an important source of food. They feed many animals. Whales, bears, and birds eat fish. So do turtles, raccoons, and snakes. And so do we! Fish are good for our health.

Fish also make good pets. They are fun to watch. And they are easy to care for.

 Up to 32,000 kinds of fish live on Earth. That's a lot more than most other kinds of animals.

Some fish are in danger of dying out. Overfishing is one reason. Too many fish are being caught for food. Rivers, lakes, and oceans have also been polluted. That harms fish too. People are working to protect fish and their homes. That way, these animals can keep swimming safely in our waters.

Trash in this river is killing fish.

Glossary

breed To come together to make babies.

carnivore A meat-eating animal.

cold-blooded An animal whose body temperature matches the air around it.

fertilize To make eggs ready to become a baby.

gills Body parts an animal uses to breathe underwater.

herbivore An animal that eats only plants.

omnivore An animal that eats plants and animals.

predator An animal that hunts other animals.

scales Overlapping plates that cover a fish's body.

scavenger An animal that eats dead animals.

school A group of fish that swim together.

Read More

Hibbert, Clare. *Fish.* Really Weird Animals. Mankato, Minn.: Arcturus Pub., 2011.

Kaspar, Anna. *What's a Fish?* All About Animals. New York: PowerKids Press, 2013.

Schreiber, Anne. *Sharks!* National Geographic Readers. Washington, D.C.: National Geographic, 2008.

Websites

EPA's Fish Kids Website: FishKids: US EPA
http://water.epa.gov/learn/kids/fishkids/index.cfm

The Facts on Fish – National Geographic Kids
http://kids.nationalgeographic.com/kids/stories/spacescience/facts-on-fish/

Fish: Science News for Kids
http://www.sciencenewsforkids.org/tag/fish/

Index

About the Author

Michelle Levine has written and edited many nonfiction books for children. She loves learning about new things—like fish—and sharing what she's learned with her readers. She lives in St. Paul, Minnesota.